Between Lines & Hashtags

A life poetic [re]collected from 1995 to 2015

Written By C. Joi Sanchez

DEDICATION

It always seemed wrong to me to write a dedication. No matter how much I would comb through the memory of my heart, there is always someone I forget. Some name I cannot think of while writing, that lives on the tip of my tongue.

This book is more than just a book. To me, it is the culmination of lessons learned & unlearned, experiences lived, loves gained & lost, over the past twenty years of my life. It is my testament to a life I am finally in love with and proud to live every day.

So this book is dedicated to all the characters that have been a part of my story. Whether great or small, the role you have played is irreplaceable. I thank you for your support, encouragement, jokes, criticism, guidance, put-downs, let-downs, pick-me-ups, and love. Most of all, I thank you for your love.

I also dedicate this book to my sun and moon. K'hari Mosi, your gentle spirit always reminding me to be tender. Niyati-Ife Rose, your compassion always reminding me to smile, though my heart is aching. My world will always revolve around you. I hope I give you strength and make you proud.

To everyone else, you have my undying gratitude.

#LoveJoi

Photo credit:

Anthony Lewis

& Joi Sanchez

TABLE OF CONTENTS:

Introduction

Bonjour
Je m'appelle JeSansChez.
Je parle francaise un petite;
and slowly
I am learning Spanish.
Y de vez en cuando
yo hablo las palabras que yo se.

Sprinkled into my speech,
I'm a seasoned New York poet.
Some say prophet.
I say dreamer,
believing all things are possible.
Always willing to work for it.

I'm a hustler.
Selling water to whales,
pipe dreams to fiends,
and everything else in between
with these lines.
I be
picking, packing, & pushing these dreams
to support life in the machine

Sometimes I rage.
I be rebel with a cause
Raising revolutions,
these dual versions of my evolution.
I am powerful.

I am conscious

I be earth
& air
& water
I am intersection
Of concrete
& blood
& bone under concrete.
I am New York.
Child of the melting pot metropolis
I can't stop in a city that never sleeps
I stay ready.

I be Brooklyn,
Thoroughbred,
80's baby, born Cosby Kid,
though more Good Times in adolescence.
I am statistic.
World says average
while I've always been above.
I am fly.

Eagle eyes threaded red from smoke & tears.
I be black girl torn between worlds
Between lines
I find myself always having to explain,
one thing or another
When it really boils down to 1 thing.

I am grown.
I do what
& who I want
when
& how I want

And with all this love inside of me,
I will always be home.

Between He & I

[1st Love]

Photo credit: Anthony Lewis, Oct. 2012

THERE, THEY'RE, THEIR (comfort poem)

's a beautiful thing, black love.
ecause they're love.
onnected by their souls, the god body within creates perfection in the image of their love.

et, in the eyes of their love, there was [is] pain.
here are [were] regrets.
here were [are] obstacles, and theirs is a love full of trials.

o their triumphs, there were times of joy.
ays where their elaborate patterns of speech and dance had them lost in the tricks & dips in their love's
aborate dance, there was a seduction.
1 there, love is a solace, a peace;
n at home feeling in their love because there, love is home,
ven in their divided homes;
here, love is celebration.
heir love is gratitude.
here, their love is a shoulder to lean on until there isn't a leg to stand on and all that comes out is the fury in
eir words.
nd sometimes there are blows to pride,
egos, & to faces from hands that once held that face to their face and softly whispered "I love you".
nd they did, even when they loved rough.

heir love was intense because their love is / was / is tough to be in,
ere comes a point when their love is not enough,
their love becomes too much for their love to handle.

Photo credit: Christoph Carr, Eat The Cake NYC

Homemade

Dear Lover,

I brought you a present.

Couldn't afford the fancy wrapping;

the trappings of fame cause a burden

on pockets filled with hands that have nothing

to offer but holding.

Handle this with care.

For it has seen its fair share of accidents.

I doubt it can handle another break.

It is fragile.

But given proper care,

there is no limit to the love

this heart will bring you.

Thanks

Former lover,
I want to say thank you for leaving.
For giving me reason to cry.
I couldn't fathom how you'd leave when had pledged me your forever.

But that was then and this is now.
It's a new day,
I have found a new way and
a new love.

The love I had always dreamed of,
all those nights laying in your arms, in our bed.
All those times when my tongue tied up
and waterfalls would wash me into invisible.

When there was nothing more to be said,
I ran so fast and furiously from my pain
straight into arms that patiently waited.
She waited for me.

Never in the same place twice,
but always with arms open wide,
inviting me to partake.

She doesn't just embrace me, she engulfs me.
From the tips pf mu toes to the top of my head.
She is the best.
My reason for breathing.

Spark to my flame.
She drowns out my pain like a shot of Novocain
or a line of cocaine.
So high off her love, I can't feel my face.

But I can see.
She's all you said was wrong, proven right.
She is the opposite of what I ever got from you.
A cataclysm of emotion.
Sunrays warming the ocean.
She is the change of the tide.
She brings strength to my stride.
She makes everything alright,
like when I'm staring down the barrel of a shotgun, begging for life to end.
She is redemption.

She takes her time and allows me to take mine.
Gives me pause.
A reason to remain still and calm until peace comes from the pieces you broke me into.
Her love be superglue.

So former lover, I want to sincerely thank you for releasing your grasp,
letting me be free
to find this love I have found with me.

Conundrum

In the future I wonder if we will still love in this way.
A broken ship to endure the lengthy journey, I was told forever was the destination.
Must our love be a fight at every turn?
Lessons learned from scornful words with hindsight leading us further from the safety of the shore?

Why does black love feel more like a head under water without the benefit of gills?
Unable to take a breath,
accepting these blues with our black because
we have been told that's just the way our love goes?

Will these broken down cycles of apathy and counter intuitive thinking,
always be what it is like to love a black man?
Will I always be too much and not enough at the same time?
Steadily seeking an impossible balance between expectation and reality.
Hypocrisy seems to turn him on.
He's on a wild goose chase for onyx unicorns.
Looking for us.

Driven women,
we whip up home cooked gourmet dishes,
create our champagne wishes all on our own.
We're out here.
Ladies in the streets,
freaks in the sheets,
nurturers in between rocks and hard places.
We make hard choices because we chose you.

And I'm not going anywhere.
I am right here.
But I cannot stroke your ego and hold your hand;
black man, please just hold my hand.

Another question:
Why is it that kinky hair and hips translate to "complicated"?
As if you fear my complexity.
I'm being the queen I was meant to be.
The one you said you'd wish I would be
because that is what you said a "king" like you really needs.
Tell me, what is it that makes me so intimidating?

Will I always be expected to keep offering up apologies
for the unanticipated tragedy of loving me?
Can lost black girls find comfort & redemption in a heart
and not in the heat of passion?
Instead of acting for Peter Pans cloaked in black man skin.
I'm asking.
Because I need to understand.
I am tired of reliving the past.
Tired of not being enough when I've poured out my love the thousand times I've runneth over.
I am tired of being bitter by proxy of my race.
Tired of holding my anger at a steady pace,
in place of you,
my heart beats steady,
and I beat myself up for being my mother's daughter.

I am tired of rebirthing your existence yet being dismissed,
and replaced in favor of women of simplicity,
draped in shades closer to sand than soil.

Perhaps I should bury my hope, along with my heart.
Let it sprout within our seeds and flourish in the future.
Perhaps black love will bloom for them,
in bouquets smelling of sweet honeysuckle and vanilla.
Wiping the memory of the broken love from where they sprang.

Osho Taught Me

He wasn't the one that got away.
He is the one she never had.
Her white whale.
Elusivity fueled chase of stubborn passion.
It shouldn't have been a surprise when she's made a dick of herself in sake of him.
Og his heart.
Of he(art).
Her long lost lover.
He seemed to love her unlike any other.
When it appeared that no others did.
He became everything she needed.
Everything she thought she wanted.
So she did it.

She loved him.

Spread her arms wide,
opened her mouth tilting her head back as she inhaled him.
Dope leaning off each hit
of his brown candy crush.
She couldn't kick the addiction.
She lived in him, died within.
Daily focused on what more she could give.
What would be enough to justify the weight dropping like dollars in an Atlanta strip club;
Rapidly and often.
She found herself caught up debating the disparity between love and their current reality.

Questioning if love is a curse?
A burden?
A constant perpetuation of anger and mounting resentment?
A reason to be spiteful?
Smashing dishes?
A hard shove against the wall at 6 months?
A hand wrapped around the throat whilst children watch from thir cribs?

NO

Heart told her.
This is not what love is.
This is everything that love isn't:\
control,
possession,
a jaded heart acting on the pain of old callouses.

But he didn't listen.
And neither did she.
They maintained the illusion.
Stretching the canvas of their lives into the thinnest of truths.
Painting over the flaws of their delusion.
The time they wasted, insisted on kidding themselves.
Appearing around town, as happy couples should do.
As they would do;

If they were in love with each other.
Instead of 4 wandering eyes that never seem to land on one another,
till the drinks kicked in.
A singular truth echoing between them.
There's no use fighting this addiction.
Might as well,
just give in to it.

Facts

I get it.
You can't stop.
Can't let go of control.
It must be you, all the time.
The only one who decides.
I get it.
You have never been alone before;
Or been on your own before.
Why would you want your past
to keep tagging along,
riding your coat tails, stealing your shine?
Except,
you forget,
you didn't do this on your own.
You were never truly on your own.
You have me.
Always have,
always will have me here.
Whether you want me or not.
I'm staying put because contrary to your beliefs,
children need their mothers just as much.
And not even you can control that.

Photo credit: Jon Cassill

Sour Grapes

The real shame of it is
that I will write love poems for you
until the sun rises in the west and sets in the east.
In a fickle attempt to turn back time.
Unmake the oceans I still shed in silence.
Every day,
I watch the gap between us widening.
With growth spurts and short skirts.
I chase empty love affairs to fill the canyons you left behind.
Captured in polaroid.
Their faces fade in record time.
Recollections of names get mixed in with memories of our early days.
Heinekens & Jameson shots,
dancing in the dark,
brown tangled bodies.
Cigarette breaks without ashtrays during 8 hour marathons.
Like: the first time you told me you loved me.
I lived until I died at your hands.

Yet still,
I write love poems for you.
Until the sun rises in the west and sets in the east.
Until I am young again and a woman you desire.
The woman I aspire to be is the one of your dreams.
I slave away for you.
Chained to a greatness to huge to hold inside of me,
I birthed it into reality.
For you.
Only for you.

I died a little that day.
Sacrificed what was meant to be the best of us.
Lost us.
Because you said it was necessary,
I selected the worst case scenario.
Believing it was best for us,
because you said it was.
Because you said it.
Said you loved me...
And left me...
To be an eye peering through the looking glass of hindsight makes perspective skewed.
When I still write love poems for you.
I celebrate our creations.
The joys of life.
Kissing boo boos,
hugging colds into oblivion,
battling Lego robots on snow days.
Anything for a smile.
Giving all I have and finding what I don't to provide security and comfort food.
Painting trails,
hoping you will follow.
Find me home waiting for the sun to rise in the west and set in the east.
Writing love poems,
for you.

You

the saddest thing
about her,
is that she thought you were worth something.

she thought
you were one of the good ones.
even when you proved all her friends right.
when you showed your ass,
as the only place for her to lay her kisses,
she loved you more.
fought for you harder.
ran faster in hopes of catching up with that dream,
of family.
and love.
and legacy with you.

but she,
was too much
or not enough or maybe you had had enough
or she was much more than you had bargained for
thought she'd stay your bottom b*tch
even after your itch had subsided
she kept her nails well manicured if ever you needed some scratch

because she love you,
when you turned your back
she turned a cheek,
relishing in the sting of the pain,
finding her way free in the submission.
she would willingly leave herself open.
unguarded.
for you to pillage.

you who always wants the world for a dollar,
without a nickle to his name.
you,
bottom of the barrel
crab ass monkey boy
peter pan
still ain't never grow up
you lost boy
black boy
still baby-faced when you shave.
she loved you when you shaved.
said your jawline reminded her of the constellations
that still hold her childhood wishes,
which is probably why,
no matter how hard she tried
she couldn't ever fix her mouth to say no.
unable to admit when she didn't want it,
couldn't take it,
or deserved better.
i'm glad she's finally realizing she deserves better
than she's been accepting,
from you.

Fate-Fetted Rock

you dear icarus
are not the sun

you are a moon
absent of your own light
your beauty is temporary
noticed once a month

a sun
always shines
on its own
while you
dear Icarus
bathe in borrowed light
to glow

you dear Icarus
are not the sun

you are a moon
vacant of all life
without the potential
to create
to nurture
or sustain life
there is no living on you

or with you
as you
pull your disappearing acts
like clockwork
cyclically

there is no depending
on one so flaky

so void of gravity
how can you possibly
hold me down?

ever-revolving
never evolving
past presumptions
you assume
I think myself the sun
simply because
you are not

you are wrong
i am not
the sun

i am the earth
inexplicably tied to you
tide and topography shifting

under your invisible influence
yet just fine on my own.

Between
She & I
[LovHers]

Jalah

i feel unworthy of your glance
because
hope springs eternal from your smile
it's like when sunrise meets baby's laughter
an intoxicating innocence
getting me lost in the chapter & verse of your testimony
anytime you speak.
it's real.
i heal a little more
listening to a
transformative wordsmith
living in your truth inspires.
sometimes
i like to daydream in the belief that had we met sooner
we wouldn't be a disaster waiting to happen
and
i wouldn't be the next person to break your heart
even after you grant me redemption
i'm still a symphony of catastrophe
and you
a nubian queen too good for the likes of me
a life lived dangerously.
perhaps you like to flirt with death and destiny
walk tightropes of propriety till proven right
that there is no wrong way to live.

against better senses i dare steal a kiss
in back yards illuminated by envious stars
i inhale your light
as if a human defribulator
jumpstarting my heart back in to a now-now time signature
with the future as a possibility
the present a security
and the past
a distant memory.

Irony

I can't stop laughing.
The irony.
Both she & he are leos.

Lion & lioness.
With almost a decade between them,
residing in the same sexual/emotional states

And me,
Gemini in Saturn

in-between them.

Julia

i admit
i'm non-compliant with life.
stuck on the memory of a love meant to last a lifetime.
acting as if everything is just fine
but really I'm losing my mind on a slow drift to insanity.
i have empty affairs to fill the void.
pretty faces that don't mean much to me.
i build them promises of sand castles
as they bask in my hollow embrace.
i sometimes see you staring back in their faces
judging this momentary love.
the next day is always the same
washing them away with the soap
on the same brown skin on which you'd plant your kisses
reminiscing,
i watch them fade through the drain
with the hope that i can love again
the same way i once loved you.

Ashley

i still have your bracelet
i wear it on my wrist with prayer beads
praying one day soon i'll forget these
feelings i had for you
that now cause flames to consume me
anytime i see your face.
it is not the loss of the possibility of love that angers me
it is that i began to let go of the hurt i hold.
reminders of what love shouldn't be
just to be given more of the same
i feel as if i'm just the last in the long line of suckas
who have fallen victim to your game
and i know i'm smarter than this.
writing angry love poems
until you don't exist
seems like the only way
to remove you
from my memory.
even though i deleted the pictures you took for me
those images are emblazoned in my psyche.
the memory of you in sun kissed onyx skin
you shined like the moon, unaware it was meant to set
and now
whenever my eyes meet darkness i dream of you.
still dream that you care,
delicate hands stroking my tears as i shared myself with you.
so yes.....
i think you are evil....
until i figure out
how to stop
wanting to love you.

Dirty Diana

On some days
I sit by her side when she's got stars in her eyes wishing for you to come around
some days, you're all she thinks about
combining past experience with present circumstance
but it leaves the mind confused
and the libido a little less then amused
when you're in her thought's rotation.

And it isn't fair how you taunt her with your butterfly wings,
they shine in your eyes when you smile,
she says, she is always trying to make you smile
she would tickle you, if you didn't hate it
she is mesmerized by your fire, no matter the tone
she says your voice seduces her from across the room
it bellows...
        inside of her..
it echoes..
        in her darkness,
each vibration, a crack in her defenses
and i'm sure she would lay down her arms,
if you set down yours
if you'd let go of the memory
the mistakes made in a transitional state
when her life was heavy
she was still learning to carry the weight
and along you came
at a meteoric rate
seemingly uninterested in anything else but self
seeming to be jumping from one relationship into the next and she couldn't get down like that
back then

ok
yes
   i know
it wasn't that much time ago
but it was time enough for her to earn a little extra and get her shit together
so she'd have real time for you and not that bullshit that you accepted
she just wanted to be able to treat you better
but you took it as an insult, to say it was all her fault, thats more of a cop out
cause if you wanted to see her
                wouldn't you have gone with her?
taken her home, not sent her out drunken with some folks she really didn't know?
not that anything happened
but it just so happens that you never ever asked her if she knew them
i don't mean to throw salt on a wound but
its just something you should consider,
personal responsibility in the choices we make
go a long way to shaping the perception of others
but she doesn't seem to want any others
she just wants to be with you
I think she's confused, she says,
(her) heart is begging for answers
but (i) brain doesn't have a clue   what to tell her
                when   she says
her third eye's vision is clouded

when its gaze lands on you
cause
this camaraderie is so damn comfortable yet the nonchalance is
smothering
she keeps being a friend when there's clearly more between you
you keep going along, all business as usual, and i'm sure you know exactly what you do when you do what you doi
whatever it is,
please for "my friend's" sake
either go all in
or step away from the table.

Lesbehonest

My mother recently asked:
"Why are you a lesbian?"
After a laugh,
I just asked: "well where should I begin?"
Maybe because
I have decided I want a girlfriend.

And not just any girl,
I want her,
the grown girl,
standing alone on her own,
in other words,
a woman
Is not because I'm sick of men
but because I'm sick of the bullshit around me.
The clothed sword fights never cease to astound me.
Because I don't wish my pussy to experience violent sex.
Being banged out or beat up is not what I call love.
Because when I was lost and forgotten, she is who found me.
When he said I was worthless, she said that I was worthy.
Because he feeds off of me, so when I am hungry,
only a feast of the sweetest fruit can restore me.
I want someone I don't need to explain my moods to.
That will ride the monthly wave of emotions, holding my hand in silent solidarity.
Forming symbiotic connections through chocolate and chic flicks.
Someone that it's okay to for me to cry with, for no reason at all,
she will become my wall, damning outsiders,
protecting the treasure of my queendom.
I want her to be my partner
Because sometimes I want be a fool,
and fall in love if I want to,
Because no love compares to that of a woman &
I deserve to have my heart handled with care and compassion.
I want someone who will share my passions
not look at me like I'm an addict cause I drool over the latest pair of Steve Maddens.
Someone who understands that sometimes shit happens.
And though this road we travel may be laid with the brick of good intentions,
sometimes I slip, so when I come groveling in shame,
she'll remind me we're all human & it's okay to make mistakes.
Because I have mommy issues and a tendency to require unconditional love
without my partner being executioner, jury & judge.
I want her because she is a verb all her own.
Pure poetry in motion when her hips sail smoothly in line with well sculpted muscular legs in those heels!.
Oooooh lawd!
Takes my breath away!
The way she pulls my hand to her waist to dance with her
Feeling heat is fine but sweat is sweet when the source is divine.
Because I want someone I can love with my mind.
Someone who will find it fine if I take my time getting to know her,
helping to grow her and myself.
Because mother,
I want a lover
who knows my wealth is hidden beneath layers of hurt,
so she is an archeologist digging deeper,
past skin to shoulder height holes of despair.

She digs until she sees the light inside my soul,
Spins prose into gold, healing the old wounds with the power she holds
She knows my time is valuable, so she doesn't waste a millisecond with small talk.
Her ideas are big and bold!
She's a woman who knows how and when to take control.
Her knowing for stronger am I .
This master Jedi, the force is strong in her.
Just a little stronger and
she could fight the voice that says this love is wrong for her.

Because my energy doesn't know its place,
because sex and gender don't always occupy traditional space.
And I think it's okay to express love however you feel it.
For a person it is real with.
Because I want to love her, she who asks for nothing in return.
The one with the sad eyes, refusing to acknowledge how loud her heart cries out to me,
through late night conversation in shared sheets,
with no indecency, she makes love to me with her vocal tones & melodies.
She who has been battered, bruised, broken and burned.
I want to love her for as long as the world turns,
no matter how long I must wait for my turn,
because I know from that moment on I will be her first,
her last, her everything.
And she will bring the spring to this endless winter I call a heart.
Mother, please stop speaking as if this is blasphemy
Maybe I'm a lesbian because that's the only word you have for me.
And I won't fault you for what you don't know.
I'll only ask you love me anyway because so many others won't.

Bicuriosity

i think its time that i admit,
while i may love every minute if it,
our time might be at an end
that maybe it best to not be more than friends,
i mean just friends,
no benefits
because
i was starting to believe you were heaven sent
and i can feel that way alone.
i'm also unsure if i am okay playing second fiddle on my own dates
and i know you said you don't want to date anyone,
that all you want is to have some fun.
with me.
thats okay,
just dont get mad when i don't call you for a few days
or look at you the same when i know he's had you today.
 don't complain that i'm not engaging enough,
as if i should share my intimacies with one not interested in learning my heart.
see with me lust is not connected to love,
so all that romantic shit gets saved for someone
who can appreciate it
who is
open to being loved,
and even more returning it
openly
see i can't agree
to be a part of the white girl wasted secret lesbian society
i don't see why you cant just embrace your queerness and admit you like some variety.
in your life.
no judgements
no shade
i'm just saying
i'm not about that life no more.
i been busted through my closet door,
and stepped into my truth.
i am living proof
that no one cares if you don't
so stop saying you will when you won't.
don't oblige me in fantasy
if the minute you're alone with me,
its not comfortable to be holding my hand in city streets,
or cuddle up next to me
or kiss me goodbye
then kiss me goodbye.

this poem is not about hetero-normalcy
it's about you and I
and all the reasons
i can no longer be your secret
adventure
thrill ride
good time,
anything more than a one night
hit(h)er & quit(h)er

see you later sister
"catch you on the flip side"
or perhaps next lifetime
when you know what you want
and are ready for it
when you can express your sexuality and not feel shameful for it
when i can be someone you adore
when you're ok being my cherie amour
and we don't have to hide.
until then,
only hit me for a good time,
a one night.
a forehead kiss
and "see you next time".

Les-Being Lessons

here are 10 things I have learned from being a lesbian:

1. I will always lose a friend reading this poem. As if you don't know me, you will drop off like shadows in the dark. And it is okay, you probably weren't meant to stay in my life too long anyway. Peace be with you.
2. There is little I can do to stop some women for hating my cis-privilege, she'll hate me for the children i had with a man. Her mind unable to understand that men are also human, and lovable. How I was once young, and dumb, and in love with one and don't regret a minute of it. So fuck it, I gotta choose my battles and my motherhood will never invalidate my womanhood.
3. Unbeknownst to me the woman falling all over herself in love with the instant family I offer. With me she can have "it" all and keep her bikini beach body, all that's left to do is fall in love. I must beware the women with holes in their heart, trying to fill them with my womb.
4. Sooner or later some man emerges from the woodworks just dying to be my wingman. In his mind he can take home his fill of my sloppy seconds. I'll let him live his fantasy for a while before I mention my ferocious appetite and that I always scrape my plate.
5. On the other hand there will always be a man hating me for my abilities because the girl he has his eye has her eye on me. The ego of patriarchal constructs of men cannot withstand the smack of my lady balls. I've already won, so I learn to walk away.
6. Remember, remember the 5th of November, the 8th of September, the 10th of January and all the other birthdays of friends no longer with me because someone at some time convinced them their love was unhealthy or they were unworthy of love. I speak their births when I can no longer speak their names, and hope that anyone feeling the same, can hear how much you would be missed if you succumb to the ignorance of others. Know you are valid and worthy of this love.
7. My kids don't care who or how I love. Long as I live and love them. Long as they see me happy, they are happy. Who says that's not normal?
8. There is always some woman calling herself bisexual, really just bi-curious, has no idea where she fits in that will follow at my feet like a lost puppy. Don't get sucked in by the cuteness, leave that little bitch where she is before she is a decision I regret along with the bottle of Jameson just to forget her. I can't tell you who you are. That's a journey for yourself.
9. Blood is indeed thicker than water. But water will wash you clean and in water we see ourselves reflected as beautiful. So it's okay to see family as relative since they act like they don't remember how much I love cartoons and warm apple pie. I longer need waste my breath explaining why you should love me. If the earth is 70% water as is my body, maybe that's why we make ourselves into family.
10. Knowledge is essential because women like to talk. So you better know something, our all night whiskey fueled intellectual stimulation be foreplay so make learning your forte if you want to get in the panties, cause women like to talk more than anything. Sapiosexuals be my favorite.

she's your mama,
so believe me when i say she's been here and done it
before.
my mom
didn't understand a lot about me
when i was outed to her but,

with time
and patience
and love,
so much love,
now she does.
or at least pretends to
understand

they're never going to get it.
and they don't need to.
all they need to do is still love you.
so maybe

you don't bring up details
of what you did last night
on the drive home from the airport
you make small talk
put on michael jackson,
you still love mj
and dance around
why you didn't bring your lover home for the holidays.

instead when you visit
you recreate high school
holing yourself up in the guest bedroom
on the phone.
giggling like once upon a time.
when she feels out the loop
and starts to be embarrassing
rush off the phone
and don't explain why you couldn't wait two more days
to have the phone call in person
because you did come to visit her.
apologize for wasting your little bit of time together.
let her pick the movie,
finish cooking the mac & cheese she loves
the only thing she never taught you to make
other than this strange love you like.

525,600 minutes

525,600 minutes
525,000 moments so dear
525,600 minutes
this is how i measure
a year in my life

for the last 525,600 minutes
her love has permeated my every thought
shifting my view
stripping the blinders off my head.
i mean she blind-sided me
i wasn't looking for love
love just found me looking pa nub
at a kink party
only interested in a companion for the night
maybe cook them breakfast before i'd leave in the morning..
i was focused on setting a personal record
for most one night stands in a weekend
but by weeks end she had me hoping she'd call me back
for a late dinner and reggae band,
split mussels and glasses of white wine
a long tour of my old hood now her new hood
its amazing how much we had in common and
how she seemed to replicate the stars on earth that night she
caught me hook line and sinker,
without notice of time slipping away
we always seem to let the day get away from us
so we can be alone. and now

525,600 minutes
525,000 moments so dear
525,600 minutes
this is how i measure
a year in my life

it is few and far between
when i talk about love
that i set out to write things like these
love poems
cause she loves my poems
even the please don't love me love poems
so it's real when i write her
a pour out my soul poem
gushing my love for her.
we be cutest couple ever
vomiting all over ourselves
with how gay we be
or laughing our asses off at
how she jokes on me
like this is a snap contest
but i love her honesty
its rough the way i like it,
never failing to break me open

yet hold me together on some super glue shit.
if i am indeed superwoman
then she is the s on my chest
branded with no sign of fading away.
i hope her love don't fade away cause for the last

525,600 minutes
525,000 moments so dear
525,600 minutes
this is how i measure
a year in my life

like how love knows how to handle my brain
often rearranges her schedule
to hear my thoughts
she is never an after thought
and frankly
after all those thots
its a miracle to find that real women still exist
in the last year
i have learned how little i am without her
how it is better that i listen to her
and dont doubt her magic
cause i been under her spell
mistaken for bruja
she is pinoy descended from healers
and oh has she has healed me in the last
525,600 minutes
with
525,000 moments so dear
525, 600 minutes
i'm so happy to have shared this year of my life.

Normal

i gave up normal
at the tender age of 6
when i kissed a boy
and i liked it
but he didn't like me as much
because black girls
weren't in style yet.
it was the early 90's
and i was 1 of 10 of us in school
and being pretty for a black girl
was normal.
i decided
i wanted to be beautiful.

i gave up normal
the first time
i saw my mother
decked out to the 9's
in all her disco diva splendor.
i was 9 years old
going back stage
at madison square garden
boppin in the dressing room
to KC & The Sunshine Band
watching her face get beat
she
transformed into superhuman
into living goddess
and i found my religion in music
screaming from the side stage.

i gave up chasing normal
when i chose to chase
shots of tequila
with more tequila.
at 17, i would dust off my dance shoes
prove those lessons my grandmother paid for did not go to waste
he
would hold me by my waist
dancing on 2's like old cubans
clapping in time to the congas
we'd dip and swirl across the floor
till i couldn't tell
if i was in love
or simply drunk
because blacking out was normal.
i wanted to know the difference
when i grew up
i knew that everything i wanted
would never be normal.

After-Word

Photo credit: Anthony Lewis, Aug. 201!

Joi Sanchez, also known as JTheGodIs, is awesome on two legs. As a multi-disciplinary artist Joi draws on social issues and personal lessons to engage audiences through visual and performance art. After studying film photography at NYU in her youth, she developed herself as a visual learning painting styles through on on one mentorships. A natural performance artist, Joi developed a unique sound and voice though trial & error, studying under some of the top emcees and vocalist in the world.

She believes to create & to love are revolutionary acts which she applies in her freestyle approach to poetry and music. Since 2013 she has been a featured performer at venues across the country including BB Kings, The Counting Room & Arlene's Grocery. She currently resides in Harlem, NY influencing the minds of the youth as a teaching artist with various non-profit art organizations throughout New York City. Founder of Art LovHer, she curates monthly artist salons as well as quarterly recorded jam sessions at Funkadelic Studios cultivating community among independent artists. Find out more about her at www.jthegodis.wordpress.com.

Thank You

#lovejo

Made in the USA
Middletown, DE
23 August 2022

72026613R00024